MIGHTY MACHINES IN ACTION

Helicopters

by Rebecca Pettiford

BELLWETHER MEDIA • MINNEAPOLIS, MN

Note to Librarians, Teachers, and Parents:

Blastoff! Readers are carefully developed by literacy experts and combine standards-based content with developmentally appropriate text.

Level 1 provides the most support through repetition of high-frequency words, light text, predictable sentence patterns, and strong visual support.

Level 2 offers early readers a bit more challenge through varied simple sentences, increased text load, and less repetition of high-frequency words.

Level 3 advances early-fluent readers toward fluency through increased text and concept load, less reliance on visuals, longer sentences, and more literary language.

Level 4 builds reading stamina by providing more text per page, increased use of punctuation, greater variation in sentence patterns, and increasingly challenging vocabulary.

Level 5 encourages children to move from "learning to read" to "reading to learn" by providing even more text, varied writing styles, and less familiar topics.

Whichever book is right for your reader, Blastoff! Readers are the perfect books to build confidence and encourage a love of reading that will last a lifetime!

This edition first published in 2018 by Bellwether Media, Inc.

No part of this publication may be reproduced in whole or in part without written permission of the publisher. For information regarding permission, write to Bellwether Media, Inc., Attention: Permissions Department, 5357 Penn Avenue South, Minneapolis, MN 55419.

Library of Congress Cataloging-in-Publication Data

Names: Pettiford, Rebecca, author.
Title: Helicopters / by Rebecca Pettiford.
Description: Minneapolis, MN : Bellwether Media, Inc., [2018] | Series: Blastoff! Readers. Mighty Machines in Action |
    Includes bibliographical references and index. | Audience: Grades K-3. | Audience: Ages 5-8.
Identifiers: LCCN 2016052734 (print) | LCCN 2017001725 (ebook) | ISBN 9781626176324
    (hardcover : alk. paper) | ISBN 9781681033624 (ebook)
Subjects: LCSH: Helicopters–Juvenile literature.
Classification: LCC TL716.2 .P48 2018 (print) | LCC TL716.2 (ebook) | DDC 629.133/352–dc23
LC record available at https://lccn.loc.gov/2016052734

Editor: Christina Leighton   Designer: Steve Porter

Printed in the United States of America, North Mankato, MN.

Table of Contents

LIFE-SAVING FLIGHT

Help has arrived! A helicopter is here to take someone to the hospital.

rotor blades

Its **rotor blades** spin fast as it lifts into the sky.

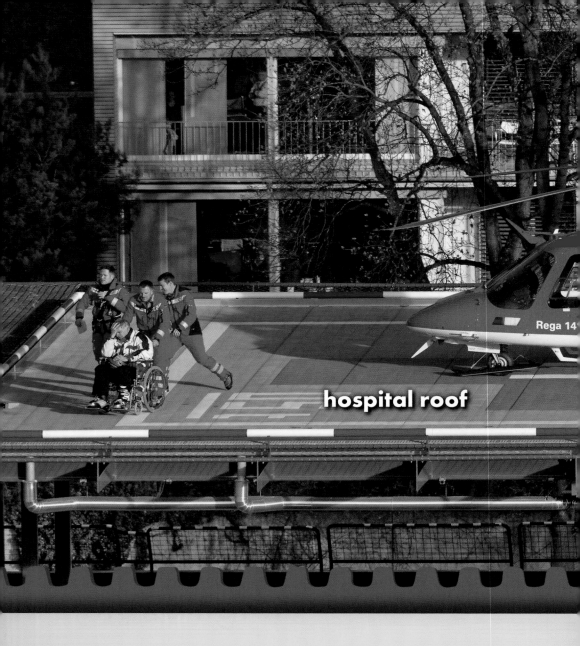

hospital roof

The helicopter zooms through the air. It lands on the hospital's roof.

The helicopter arrives in time
to help save a life!

Helicopters have many jobs. Firefighters use them to help put out fires.

The military uses them to carry **cargo** and troops. The machines also fight enemies.

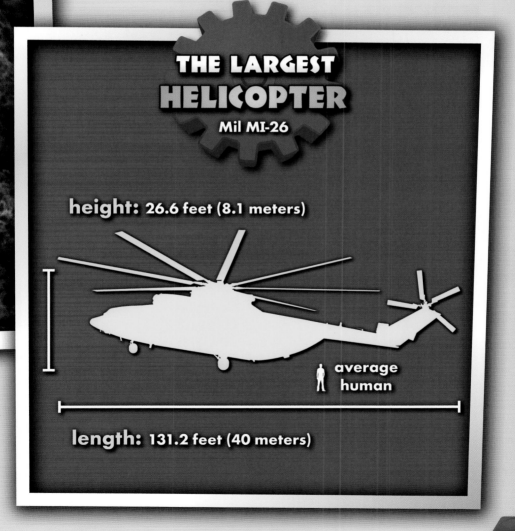

THE LARGEST
HELICOPTER
Mil MI-26

height: 26.6 feet (8.1 meters)

average
human

length: 131.2 feet (40 meters)

Some helicopters **rescue** people who are lost.

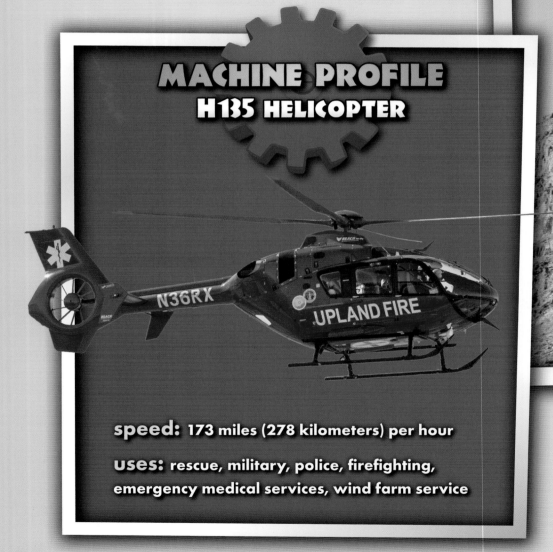

MACHINE PROFILE
H135 HELICOPTER

speed: 173 miles (278 kilometers) per hour

uses: rescue, military, police, firefighting, emergency medical services, wind farm service

Others are used to take **aerial** photographs and videos.

Helicopters fly up and down. They also go forward, backward, and sideways.

cockpit

pilot

Pilots control helicopters in **cockpits**. The pilots must use their hands and feet to steer!

A helicopter engine is powerful. The engine spins the **main rotor** on top.

main rotor

engine

blades

The spinning blades catch air. This lifts the helicopter up.

A **tail rotor** is in the back of the helicopter. It balances the helicopter.

tail rotor

Without its tail rotor, a
helicopter goes in circles!

skids

Helicopters use wheels or **skids** to land. These machines touch down on many surfaces.

They can land on **concrete**, snow, and even water!

IDENTIFY A
HELICOPTER

main rotor

rotor blades

cockpit

tail rotor

Sometimes, helicopters do not even need to land. They can **hover** in midair.

These machines are hard workers. They zip across the sky every day!

Glossary

aerial—from the air

cargo—something that is carried by a helicopter

cockpits—the parts of helicopters where the pilots sit

concrete—a hard, strong building material made with cement, sand, rocks, and water

hover—to stay in one place in the air

main rotor—the part on a helicopter that turns the top rotor blades

pilots—people who fly helicopters

rescue—to save someone from harm or danger

rotor blades—the long blades on a helicopter that turn around a central point and create lift

skids—landing gear on a helicopter that looks like tubes or skis

tail rotor—the part at the back of a helicopter that helps steer and balance

To Learn More

AT THE LIBRARY

Carr, Aaron. *Helicopters*. New York, N.Y.:
AV2 by Weigl, 2016.

Meister, Cari. *Helicopters*. Minneapolis,
Minn.: Jump!, 2014.

Willis, John. *Helicopters*. New York, N.Y.:
AV2 by Weigl, 2017.

ON THE WEB

Learning more about helicopters
is as easy as 1, 2, 3.

1. Go to www.factsurfer.com.

2. Enter "helicopters" into the search box.

3. Click the "Surf" button and you will see a
   list of related web sites.

With factsurfer.com, finding more
information is just a click away.

Index

The images in this book are reproduced through the courtesy of: Just2shutter, front cover (sky), pp. 12-13 (sky background); pidjoe, front cover (helicopter); Natali Glado, p. 4; Sky_Blue, pp. 4-5; Erix2005, pp. 6-7; GENE BLEVINS/ REUTERS/ Newscom, pp. 8-9; Steve Porter, p. 9 (helicopter graphic); betto rodrigues, p. 10; A.P.S. (UK)/ Alamy, pp. 10-11; vaalaa, pp. 12-13; pio3, pp. 12-13 (pilot); Richair, pp. 14-15 (engine); Peter Lovás, pp. 14-15 (helicopter); Oil and Gas Photographer, p. 16; Studioimagen73, pp. 16-17; ksl, pp. 18-19; tomatto, p. 19 (helicopter); Andrey Khachatryan, p. 19 (rotor); Imfoto, p. 19 (tail rotor); guvendemir, pp. 20-21.